How Can I Develop a
Christian Conscience?

THE CRUCIAL QUESTIONS SERIES
BY R. C. SPROUL

CRUCIAL
QUESTIONS
No. | 15

How Can I Develop a Christian Conscience?

R.C. Sproul

ℝ *Reformation Trust*   A DIVISION OF LIGONIER MINISTRIES, ORLANDO, FL

How Can I Develop a Christian Conscience?

© 2013 by R. C. Sproul
Published by Reformation Trust Publishing
a division of Ligonier Ministries
421 Ligonier Court, Sanford, FL 32771
Ligonier.org   ReformationTrust.com

Printed in North Mankato, MN
Corporate Graphics
October 2013
First edition

Cover design: Gearbox Studios
Interior design and typeset: Katherine Lloyd, The DESK

All Scripture quotations are from *The Holy Bible, English Standard Version*®, copyright © 2001 by Crossway Bibles, a publishing ministry of Good News Publishers. Used by permission. All rights reserved.

Library of Congress Cataloging-in-Publication Data

Sproul, R. C. (Robert Charles), 1939-
  How can I develop a Christian conscience? / R.C. Sproul.
    pages cm. -- (The crucial questions series ; No. 15)
  ISBN 978-1-56769-327-0
1. Conscience--Religious aspects--Christianity. 2. Christian ethics.
I. Title.
  BJ1278.C66S67 2013
  241'.1--dc23
                        2013014033

Contents

Chapter One

THE QUESTION OF
CONSCIENCE

I t is vitally important for Christians to consider the issue of conscience. In the classical view, the conscience was thought to be something that God implanted within our minds. Some people even went so far as to describe the conscience as the voice of God within us. The idea was that God created us in such a way that there was a link between the sensitivities of the mind and the conscience with its built-in responsibility to God's eternal laws. For example, consider the law of nature that the Apostle Paul says is written on our hearts. There was a sensitivity of conscience long before Moses came down from Mount Sinai with the tablets of stone.

The famous philosopher Immanuel Kant was agnostic with respect to man's ability to reason from this world to the transcendence of God. Even so, he offered what he called a moral argument for the existence of God that was based on what he called a universal sense of oughtness implanted in the heart of every human being. Kant believed that everyone carried with them a genuine sense of what one ought to do in a given situation. He called this the categorical imperative. He believed there are two things that fill the soul with an ever-new and growing wonder and reverence: the starry heavens above and the moral law within. This is important to note because even in the realm of secular philosophy, there has historically been an awareness of conscience.

Historically and classically, the conscience was seen to be our link to the transcendent ethic that resides in God. But with the moral revolution of our culture, a different approach to conscience has emerged, and this is what is called the relativistic view. This is indeed the age of relativism, where values and principles are considered to be mere expressions of the desires and interests of a given group of people at a given time in history. We repeatedly hear that there are no absolutes in our world today.

Yet if there are no absolute, transcendent principles, how do we explain this mechanism that we call the conscience? Within a relativistic framework, we see the conscience being defined in evolutionary terms: people's subjective inner personalities are reacting to evolutionary advantageous taboos imposed upon them by their society or by their environment. Having reached a period in our development when these taboos no longer serve to advance our evolution, they can be discarded with nary a thought of the consequences.

As a professor some years ago, I counseled a college girl who was overtaken with a sense of profound guilt because she had indulged in sexual activities with her fiancé. She explained to me that she had spoken of her guilt to a local pastor. He counseled her that the way to get over her guilt was to recognize the source of it. He reasoned that she had done nothing wrong; rather, her feelings of guilt were a result of her having been a victim of living in a society ruled by a puritan ethic. He explained that she had been conditioned by certain sexual taboos that made her feel guilty when she shouldn't and that what she had done was a mature, responsible expression of her own emerging adulthood.

Yet she came to me weeping and exclaimed that she still felt guilty. I told her it is possible for a person to feel guilty because they have an uneasy, disquieted conscience about something that is actually not a violation of God's law, but that in this case she had broken the law of God, and she should rejoice that she felt guilty, because pain, as uncomfortable as it is to us, is an important for our health. In the physical realm, the feeling of pain signals that there is something wrong with the body. Spiritually speaking, the pain of guilt, can signal to us that something is wrong with our souls. There is a remedy for that and it's the same one that the church has always offered, namely, forgiveness. Real guilt requires real forgiveness.

This woman's problem illustrates the conflict between the traditional understanding of sin and conscience and the new concept of conscience. This new concept sees it merely as an evolutionary, societal-conditioning process that is a result of imposed taboos. How does the Christian sort all of this out? Is there a biblical view of conscience?

The Hebrew term translated into the English as "conscience" occurs in the Old Testament, but very sparsely. However in the New Testament, there seems to be a fuller awareness of the importance of the function of conscience in the Christian life. The Greek word for conscience appears in the New Testament thirty-one times, and it seems to have a two-fold dimension, as the medieval scholars argued. It involves the idea of accusing as well as the idea of excusing. When we sin, the conscience is troubled. It accuses us. The conscience is the tool that God the Holy Spirit uses to convict us, bring us to repentance, and to receive the healing of forgiveness that flows from the gospel.

But there is also the sense in which this moral voice in our minds and hearts also tells us what is right. Remember that the Christian is always a target for criticisms that may or may not be valid. Even within the Christian community, there are wide differences of opinion regarding which behaviors are pleasing to God and which aren't. One man approves dancing; another disapproves of it. How do we know who is correct?

We see in the New Testament that the conscience is not the final ethical authority for human conduct because the conscience is capable of change. Whereas God's principles don't change, our consciences vacillate and develop.

These changes can be positive or negative. For example, the prophets in the Old Testament thundered God's judgment upon the people of Israel who had grown accustomed to sin. One of the great indictments that came upon Israel in the days of King Ahab was that they had grown so numb and accustomed to evil that the people tolerated King Ahab's wickedness. Hardness of the heart had set in. The consciences of the Israelites were seared and calloused. Think about this reality in your life, about the ideals that you had as a child. Consider the pangs of conscience that may have intruded into your life when you first experimented with certain things that you knew were wrong. You were overwhelmed and shaken. Perhaps you even became physically ill. But the power of sin can erode the conscience to the point where it becomes a faint voice in the deepest recesses of your soul. By this, our consciences become hardened and callous, condemning what is right and excusing what is wrong.

It's interesting that we can always find someone who will give an articulate and persuasive defense for the ethical legitimacy of some of the activities that God has judged to be an outrage to Him. As humans, our ability to defend ourselves from moral culpability is quite developed and nuanced. We become a culture in trouble when we begin to call evil good and good evil. To do that, we must distort the conscience, and, in essence, make man the final authority in life. All one has to do is to adjust his conscience to suit his ethic. Then we can live life with peace of mind, thinking that we are living in a state of righteousness.

The conscience can be sensitized in a distorted way. Remember, the relativistic and evolutionary view of conscience is built on the principle that it is a subjective response to taboos imposed upon it by society. Though I don't believe that such a view is finally compelling, I have to acknowledge that there is an element of truth in that view. We recognize that people can have highly sensitized consciences, not because they are being informed by the Word of God but because they have been informed by man-made rules and regulations. In some Christian communities, the test of one's faith, is whether or not a person dances. If one grows up in this environment and decides to dance in the future, what happens? Usually, the person is overcome with guilt for having danced. How should you respond to that? Would you tell the person that dancing isn't a sin, that his conscience has been misinformed? That might be a normal approach, but such a response may be problematic for this reason: the conscience can excuse when it ought to be accusing, and it also can accuse when it should be excusing.

We must remember that acting against conscience is sin. Martin Luther, at the Diet of Worms, was in moral agony because he stood alone against the leaders of the church and state and they demanded that he recant of his writings. But Luther was convinced that his writings conformed to the Word of God, and so in that moment of crisis he said, "I can't recant. My conscience is held captive by the word of God and to act against conscience is neither right nor safe." That was not a principle that Martin Luther invented for the occasion at the Diet of Worms. It is a New Testament principle: "For whatever does not proceed from faith is sin" (Rom. 14:23).

If a person is raised in an environment that has persuaded him that it's a sin to read philosophy but he reads philosophy anyway, then he is sinning. Why? Is it because reading philosophy is a sin? No, it is because he is doing something that he believes is a sin. If we do something that we think is sin, even if we are misinformed, we are guilty of sin. We are guilty of doing something we believe to be wrong. We act against our consciences. That is a very important principle. Luther was correct in saying, "It is neither right nor safe to act against conscience."

On the other hand, we have to remember that acting according to conscience may sometimes be sin as well. If the conscience is misinformed, then we seek the reasons for this misinformation. Is it misinformed because the person has been negligent in studying the Word of God? God has been pleased to reveal His principles to us, and He requires that each Christian master those principles so that the conscience is informed. I may think that it's fine to indulge in a particular activity that God absolutely prohibits, and I cannot say to God on the last day, "I didn't know that you would be displeased with this form of behavior. My conscience didn't accuse me, and I acted according to my conscience." In such a case you acted according to a conscience that was ignorant of God's Word that was available to you and that you were called to study and be diligent in your understanding thereof.

We must return to the first principle. For the Christian, the conscience is not the ultimate authority in life. We are called to have the mind of Christ, to know the good, and to have our minds and hearts trained by God's truth so that when the moment of pressure comes, we will be able to stand with integrity.

Chapter Two

THE CREATION ORDINANCES

In this chapter, we'll consider an important element of Christian ethics that is often overlooked. We must consider what theologians have called creation ordinances. Let me begin with a statement that may surprise you: Christians in every society, at all times, and in all ages always live under law. Your surprise at that statement may be that we are repeatedly told in the New Testament that we are no longer under law but under grace. And I certainly put great emphasis on the central importance of grace in understanding Christian ethics. Nevertheless, all of the grace that comes to us in the New Testament does not entirely eliminate the fact that we live under law.

We are New Testament Christians, and if we look at things in biblical categories, we see that the Bible is divided into different testaments. A testament is a covenant. We speak of the old covenant and the new covenant, the Old Testament and the New Testament. But we must take that a bit further. What is the essence of a covenant? In its simplest terms, a covenant is an agreement or contract between two or more persons. Every covenant contains within it certain benefits and promises, and every covenant includes legal requirements or laws. Even the new covenant, the New Testament, is a covenant with laws. Jesus said, "If you love me, you will keep my commandments" (John 14:15). Yes, the curse of the law has been satisfied in Christ. We have been redeemed from it, but that doesn't mean that now, as Christians, we are free from all obligations to our God. There are laws in the New Testament just as there are laws in the Old Testament.

As a Christian, I am a member of a covenant community, which we call the church. Every member of the

Christian church participates in the new covenant, just as every member of the household of Israel in the Old Testament participated in the old covenant. Jew and Christian alike are covenant people, but what about the rest of the world? What about the millions of people on this planet who are not members of the Christian church or members of a Jewish community? Are they in a covenant relationship with God? The answer is yes.

All men, everywhere, are participants in a covenant relationship with God even if they never join the Christian church or the Jewish commonwealth. The first covenant that God made with mankind was with Adam, who represented the entire human race. In that covenant, the covenant of creation, God entered into a contractual relationship with all human beings. By nature, every descendant of Adam belongs to the covenant of creation. This may not be a relationship of grace, but it is a relationship nonetheless. The laws that God gave in creation remain binding on all men. It doesn't matter if they are religious, members of the household of Israel, or members of a local church.

There is a certain body of moral legislation that God gives to all men, and it is that body of law that we are concerned with under the rubric of the covenant of creation.

What kind of ordinances are included in the covenant of creation? We'll look at a few of the precepts and principles that God built into human relationships in the very beginning. In the garden of Eden, God established the sanctity of life. Before Moses received the Ten Commandments at Mount Sinai, the human race knew that it is wrong to murder. The prohibition against murder is set forth in the law of creation. It is a creation ordinance. Another principle is the sanctity of marriage. Marriage is not something that has arbitrarily developed over time. It isn't that human beings, by nature, were disinclined toward monogamous relationships, and later, through societal taboos, were manipulated to form the unit of family that functions as the stable, center point of any society. The sanctity of marriage is given by God in creation. Incidentally, this is one of the reasons why the church recognizes the validity of civil marriage ceremonies. We do not reserve the right to perform marriages to the church alone. We acknowledge the just estate of marriage that is set forth by the officers and magistrates of the civil state because marriage is not a uniquely ecclesiastical ordinance. It's a creation ordinance. The state not only has the right but also the responsibility to regulate these matters.

How does this apply to our daily lives as Christians? As Christian people, we live under more than one covenant. As members of the body of Christ, we are also still members of the body of creation; we are still under the laws and the ordinances that God imposed on man as man.

We need to understand that creation ordinances transcend the limits of the particular laws that we find within the New Testament church. That means that the laws of creation go beyond the confines of the Christian church. One of the most embattled issues in our society is the relationship between the church and civil legislation. The covenant of creation establishes the basis by which the church can address moral matters in the wider secular culture.

We believe in the separation of church and state, so some people say that it is not the part of the church's business to address moral matters outside of the church. But we are not talking about imposing ecclesiastical ordinances on the wider culture. It certainly would be a violation of the separation of church and state if we became a lobby group and tried to impose the celebration of the Lord's Supper on every resident of the United States. We can't impose a legal requirement on people who live outside of the covenant framework in which that particular mandate came, namely, the new covenant in Christ. But what about when the state is not fulfilling its obligation under God of carrying out the creation ordinances? The church is called to be the prophetic voice of God in a given society and call attention to the fact that all men are under the authority of the creation mandates.

What if people are atheists and don't recognize the laws of creation? Remember, atheism doesn't nullify the laws that God has given to man. The covenant of creation is inescapable. One cannot just repudiate it and step out of it. We can break the covenant, but we cannot annul the covenant of creation. So, Christians are called upon to be voices in favor of maintaining and preserving the sanctity of life, the sanctity of marriage, the sanctity of labor, and yes, even the sanctity of the Sabbath day. These are laws that apply to all men in every age, place, and culture.

How many times have you heard it said that "you can't legislate morality?" That's been stated so often that it has become a cliché in our culture. It's interesting to note that the very phrase itself has undergone a kind of strange metamorphosis. The original sense was that you can't end sin by simply passing laws that prohibit it. If we could, all we would have to do is legislate against every conceivable sin, and the legislation itself would get rid of evil. But we know better than that. We know that people sin in spite of the fact that laws tell them not to. In fact, Paul himself expounds this idea in the book of Romans, where he says that there's a certain sense in which the presence of law causes fallen people to sin with greater abandon.

But the statement that you can't legislate morality has now come to mean that it's wrong for the government to ever pass legislation of a moral nature. Unfortunately, I've heard very few people think through the implications of this idea. What would happen in a society if no moral legislation was allowed to be passed? There wouldn't be much left for the legislators to do. What could they legislate? The state flag? The state bird? The speed limit? But how a person drives their car on the highway is a moral matter. If I recklessly endanger another person's life because of my own selfish interests, that has moral implications. Stealing another person's property has moral implications. If we can't legislate morality, we can't have laws against murder, against stealing, against false weights and measures, or against reckless behavior in public because these are all moral issues. Of course, if you think it through, you realize that moral issues are at the heart of all legislation. The question is not whether the state should legislate morality. The question is what morality should the state be legislating? If there's any point in our culture where we have experienced a profound crisis, it is precisely at this point. What is the guideline for the laws of the land? We've seen a significant shifts, not only in American history, but in the history of Western civilization. That shift is away from a Judeo-Christian concept of law.

Historically, even within our own history, we see three levels of law. There is what we call the eternal law; there is natural law; and finally, there is what we call positive law. Working backwards, we should understand these terms. A positive law is a particular law that appears on the books. "You may not sell falsely measured baskets of wheat in the marketplace." That's a positive law. The questions may be raised right away: "Well, why shouldn't we sell falsely weighted measures of wheat in the marketplace? Why can't we lie about the contents of the ingredients that we're selling?" Historically, we would see that this kind of selling involves a violation of certain principles. The principle here is the integrity of labor as well as the principle of the sanctity of truth.

Natural law states that in nature there are certain principles that we should never violate. But why? Just because nature says it's wrong? No. Classically and historically, Christianity has said that those laws that we find in nature are the external manifestations of the law of God. Remember that all true and just law is based ultimately on the character of God and His eternal being. From those eternal principles we get a reflection of God in natural law.

Finally, there are particular, positive laws enacted in this world which are to reflect the natural law. This, in turn, reflects the eternal law, so that a law is considered good or just if it corresponds ultimately to God's standards of righteousness.

We have a crisis of profound proportions in Western civilization. It's a crisis of ethical principles. In the seventeenth century and into the eighteenth century, during the Enlightenment, a tremendous reaction against biblical revelation was voiced in Europe. Confidence in a revealed source of knowledge of eternal law came to be rejected. Society tried to establish itself in a revolutionary way, basing its legal structure on natural law apart from a consideration of the revealed law of God. In fact, one of the nations that emerged at that point in history was the republic of the United States of America. There is a key phrase in our founding documents: We are endowed by our Creator with certain inalienable rights, among which are life and liberty the pursuit of happiness. The idea of the sanctity of life that is rooted and grounded in creation, is a part of the bedrock of the philosophical ethos of our nation.

But in the nineteenth century, confidence began to erode in natural law with the rise of *positivism*. Oliver Wendell Holmes, when he was an associate justice of the Supreme Court, said that law can no longer be enacted with an appeal to transcendent principles of ultimate truth. He said law merely reflects the tastes and the preferences of the current society at any given moment. Such an idea creates the legal free-for-all in which we now live, where laws are passed that are cut off from their classical foundation. Now the standard for a law is not eternal truth, or eternal principle, or the character of God, but the wishes and desires of the most powerful or most vocal majority. It's what the special interest group is able to legislate that becomes the law of the land, and when that happens, we begin to live on the basis of expediency, rather than on the basis of principle. This is the time for Christians to call attention to the *lex aeternita*, the eternal law, and that eternal law of God is manifested in *lex naturalis*, the natural law that is built into creation. This protects society from the tyranny of the human majority and places us safely under God's law.

There is a difference between rule by men and rule by law. Men make laws, but the laws they make are supposed to be subordinate to the law of God. That is the supreme norm for a society. As Christians, we need to be keenly alert to this radical change in the fabric of our own society and judicial system. We need to open our mouths and say "no" when we see our legislators legislating on the basis of expediency rather than on the basis of principle. Of course, if there's going to be a Reformation, it has to start with us. It has to start in our own lives. In the final analysis, what the culture does or does not do must not affect my responsibility to God. We are called to be a people of principle. Reformation starts when we begin to live by principle and not by expediency.

Chapter Three

THE RAZOR'S EDGE

We're in a revolution. It's not a bloody revolution or an armed revolution, but it's a revolution nevertheless. It's one that is acutely real and touches the lives of every Christian. The media labels it a moral revolution.

As Christians, we're concerned about moral issues and we see that ethics, as a science, is not something that emerges simply by evolutionary processes in nature. It is a sub-heading underneath the discipline of theology. Our culture is confused in reference to ethics and morality. In our vocabulary, you'll find that most people use the words, *ethics* and *morality* interchangeably, as if they were synonyms. But historically, that's not been the case.

The English word "ethic" or "ethics" comes from the Greek word *ethos*. The word "morals" or "morality" comes from the word *mores*. The difference is that the *ethos* of a society or culture deals with its foundational philosophy, its concept of values, and its system of understanding how the world fits together. There is a philosophical value system that is the *ethos* of every culture in the world. On the other hand, *mores* has to do with the customs, habits, and normal forms of behavior that are found within a given culture.

In the first instance, ethics is called a *normative science;* it's the study of norms or standards by which things are measured or evaluated. Morality, on the other hand, is what we would call a *descriptive science*. A descriptive science is a method to describe the way things operate or behave. Ethics are concerned with the imperative and morality is concerned with the indicative. What do we mean by that? It means that ethics is concerned with "ought-ness," and morality is concerned with "is-ness."

Ethics, or *ethos*, is normative and imperative. It deals with

what someone *ought* to do. Morality describes what someone *is* actually doing. That's a significant difference, particularly as we understand it in light of our Christian faith, and also in light of the fact that the two concepts are confused, merged, and blended in our contemporary understanding.

What has come out of the confusion of ethics and morality is the emergence of what I call "statistical morality." This is where the normal or regular becomes the normative. Here's how it works: to find out what is normal, we do a statistical survey, we take a poll, or we find out what people are actually doing. For example, suppose we find out that a majority of teenagers are using marijuana. We then come to the conclusion that at this point in history, it is normal for an adolescent in the American culture to indulge in the use of marijuana. If it is normal, we deem it to be good and right.

Ultimately, the science of ethics is concerned with what is right, and morality is concerned with what is accepted. In most societies, when something is accepted, it is judged to be right. But oftentimes, this provokes a crisis for the Christian. When the normal becomes the normative, when what *is* determines what *ought* to be, we may as Christians find ourselves swimming hard against the cultural current.

The Christian concept of ethics is on a collision course with much of what is being expressed as morality. This is because we do not determine right or wrong based on what everybody else is doing. For example, if we study the statistics, we will see that all men at one time or another lie. That doesn't mean that all men lie all the time, but that all men have indulged in lying at some time or another. If we look at that statistically, we would say that one hundred percent of people indulge in dishonesty, and since it's one hundred percent universal, we should come to the conclusion that it's perfectly normal for human beings to tell lies. Not only normal, but perfectly human. If we want to be fully human, we should encourage ourselves in the direction of lying. Of course, that's what we call a *reductio ad absurdum* argument, where we take something to its logical conclusion and show the folly of it. But that's not what usually occurs in our culture. Such obvious problems in developing a statistical morality are often overlooked. The Bible says that we lean toward lying, and yet we are called to a higher standard. As Christians, the character of God supplies our ultimate *ethos* or ethic, the ultimate framework by which we discern what is right, good, and pleasing to Him.

When it comes to every Christian's duty to pursue righteousness—to pursue right ethics—there are two significant issues. The first issue is to know what the good is, to understand with the mind what God requires and what pleases Him. But let's suppose that we have a clear and sharp understanding of God's law and we know with certainty what He requires of us. Unfortunately, that's only half the battle.

The second issue we face as Christians is to have the ethical courage to do what we know to be right. Let me raise a practical question: Do we always do what we know is the right thing to do? Of course not. None of us consistently does what we know we are supposed to do. It is not enough to know the good if we lack the moral courage to do what is right.

When we look at the issue of knowing what principles God approves for His people, we often encounter people who see ethical issues too simplistically. We sometimes refer to a person as being "too black and white," meaning that they have no time for intellectual nuance or gray areas. This type of person is generally considered intellectually childish, and that is indeed sometimes the case. Unfortunately, we can also go to the opposite extreme and celebrate the existence and confusion of the gray areas as an end in itself.

There are different ways of talking about gray areas in ethics. On the one hand, the gray may stand for what the Bible calls matters of behavior that are *adiaphora*. This word refers to behavior that has to do with external things that carry no particular ethical weight in and of themselves. One could say that these are morally neutral matters. There is often debate about this in Christian circles. One school of thought says there are many things about which the Bible says nothing. They would argue that in these areas, freedom of conscience should reign. On the other hand, there are those who argue strenuously that there is nothing neutral under the sun. God calls his people to live all of life for His glory; thus, there are no situations that are free from ethical reflection.

Both of those positions cannot be entirely true, but each may have some degree of merit. I am sympathetic to those who insist that we do everything to the glory of God. The Bible is clear on that. On the other hand, the Bible also tells us that certain things are *adiaphora* in and of themselves, such as meat offered to idols. This issue has no ethical bearing whatsoever when we consider it apart from anything else. What we do with the meat offered to idols is what God is concerned about.

Let's consider another example. Playing ping-pong is neither prohibited nor commanded by Holy Scripture, and playing ping-pong is morally neutral in and of itself. But a person could become addicted to playing ping-pong to such a degree that he neglects all of his daily responsibilities because he's always at the ping-pong table. In this case, ping-pong has now moved from an act that is *adiaphora* to an act that is sin.

The gray area represents what I would call the "area of ignorance." This is an area of confusion that exists in our minds about ethical principles. I understand that people who see everything in black or white categories can be annoying at times, but when it comes to ethical judgments, I am convinced that there are no gray areas in God's mind. Everything that I do of an ethical character either pleases God or it does not. But God has not specified His black-and-white will for every conceivable circumstance. There are many ethical problems that we face every day that are not easy to pigeonhole.

For example, stealing is plainly wrong according to the Bible. We also know that giving to the poor is good in the

Lord's eyes. If you ask ten Christians if it is a good thing to steal, they will all generally agree that stealing is a sin. If queried as to whether it's good to give to the poor, they would think it's charity, and that's a wonderful thing. But have you considered income taxes? This is where the government takes money from one group of people and dispenses it to another group of people. Here we have a forceful transfer of wealth from one group to another group. Is that good or evil? Is that theft or is it charity? Maybe it's not quite so easy to discern whether such a practice is right or wrong.

Friedrich Nietzsche, the famous nihilist philosopher, said the most fundamental aspect of human nature is what he described as man's intrinsic and inherent "will to power." He said that humans have a lust for conquest, and if we're to understand mankind, we have to measure man's actions in terms of this primordial, fundamental, passionate, and consuming drive to conquer other people. This will to power accounts for the violence, bloodshed, and warfare that has marred the history of civilization.

Of course, we know that a lust for dominance is sin. However, if we examine the biblical concept of man, we see that God has built into man an aspiration for significance. We have an inner drive and desire for meaningful existence, and that's a good thing. But if we take that which is good and let it be distorted so that our desire for significance becomes dominant to the point where it violates others, it crosses the line. When it's all the way across the line, it's plainly seen as wrong. But before it clearly crosses the line— when it's still in the gray area—that's when we are puzzled.

Unless we are well equipped with the tools of divine revelation, how are we ever going to be able to discern that acute line between righteousness and wickedness? Without knowing what the God of Word says, there will be too many gray areas before us. Yet the Bible doesn't simply give us one or two principles, but many principles, so it takes work to understand and apply what it says about ethical issues. The more principles we learn, the better our understanding of ethics will become.

Chapter Four

THE LEGALIST DISTORTION

Christians are tempted to fall prey to one of two common distortions when it comes to the law of God and ethics. These disasters that may trap the Christian who seeks to live a godly life are *legalism* and *antinomianism*. We'll explore antinomianism—"anti-lawism"—in the next chapter. In this chapter, we'll consider legalism.

Have you, as a Christian, ever been accused of legalism? That word is often bandied about in the Christian subculture incorrectly. For example, some people might call John a legalist because they view him as narrow-minded. But the term *legalism* does not refer to narrow-mindedness. In reality, legalism manifests itself in many subtle ways.

Basically, legalism involves abstracting the law of God from its original context. Some people seem to be preoccupied in the Christian life with obeying rules and regulations, and they conceive of Christianity as being a series of do's and don'ts, cold and deadly set of moral principles. That's one form of legalism, where one is concerned merely with the keeping of God's law as an end in itself.

Now, God certainly cares about our following His commandments. Yet there is more to the story that we dare not forget. God gave laws such as the Ten Commandments in the context of the covenant. First, God was gracious. He redeemed His people out of slavery in Egypt and entered into a loving, filial relationship with Israel. Only after that grace-based relationship was established did God begin to define the specific laws that are pleasing to Him. I had a professor in graduate school who said, "The essence of Christian theology is grace, and the essence of Christian ethics is gratitude." The legalist isolates the law from the

God who gave the law. He is not so much seeking to obey God or honor Christ as he is to obey rules that are devoid of any personal relationship. There's no love, joy, life, or passion. It's a rote, mechanical form of law-keeping that we call externalism. The legalist focuses only on obeying bare rules, destroying the broader context of God's love and redemption in which He gave His law in the first place.

To understand the second type of legalism, we must remember that the New Testament distinguishes between the letter of the law (its outward form) and the spirit of the law. The second form of legalism divorces the letter of the law from the spirit of the law. It obeys the letter but violates the spirit. There's only a subtle distinction between this form of legalism and the one previously mentioned.

How does one keep the letter of the law but violate its spirit? Suppose a man likes to drive his car at the minimum required speed irrespective of the conditions under which he is driving. If he is on an interstate and the minimum posted speed is forty miles per hour, he drives forty miles per hour and no less. He does this even during torrential downpours, when driving at this minimum required speed actually puts other people in danger because they have had the good sense to slow down and drive twenty miles an hour so as not to skid off the road or hydroplane. The man who insists on a speed of forty miles per hour even under these conditions is driving his car to please himself alone. Although he appears to the external observer as one who is scrupulous in his civic obedience, his obedience is only external, and he doesn't care at all about what the law is actually all about. This second kind of legalism obeys the externals while the heart is far removed from any desire to honor God, the intent of His law, or His Christ.

This second type of legalism can be illustrated by the Pharisees who confronted Jesus over healing on the Sabbath day (Matt. 12:9–14). They were concerned only with the letter of the law and avoiding anything that might look like work to them. These teachers missed the spirit of the law, which was directed against ordinary labor that is not required to maintain life and not against efforts to heal the sick.

The third type of legalism adds our own rules to God's law and treats them as divine. It is the most common and deadly form of legalism. Jesus rebuked the Pharisees at this very point, saying, "You teach human traditions as if they were the word of God." We have no right to heap up restrictions on people where He has no stated restriction.

Each church has a right to set its own policies in certain areas. For example, the Bible says nothing about soft drinks in the church's fellowship hall, but a church has every right to regulate such things. But when we use these human policies to bind the conscience in an ultimate way and make such policies determinative of one's salvation, we venture dangerously into territory that is God's alone.

Many people think that the essence of Christianity is following the right rules, even rules that are extrabiblical. For example, the Bible doesn't say that we can't play cards or have a glass of wine with dinner. We can't make these matters the external test of authentic Christianity. That would be a deadly violation of the gospel because it would substitute human tradition for the real fruits of the Spirit. We come perilously close to blasphemy by misrepresenting Christ in this way. Where God has given liberty, we should never enslave people with man-made rules. We must be careful to fight this form of legalism.

The gospel calls men to repentance, holiness, and godliness. Because of this, the world finds the gospel offensive. But woe to us if we add unnecessarily to that offense by distorting the true nature of Christianity by combining it with legalism. Because Christianity is concerned with morality, righteousness, and ethics, we can easily make that subtle move from a passionate concern for godly morality into legalism if we are not careful. But this is a supreme distortion. It's a distortion to the right rather than to the left, but distortions exist in both directions.

Closely related to this is the form of legalism that "majors in minors," of which the Pharisees were masters. Jesus said, "Woe to you, scribes and Pharisees, hypocrites! For you tithe mint and dill and cumin, and have neglected the weightier matters of the law: justice and mercy and faithfulness" (Matt. 23:23). Notice how Jesus complimented them for obeying some matters of the law. They paid their tithe. The latest report I have seen indicates that only four percent of U.S. church members tithe their income. We don't even obey God in the lesser matters, but at least the Pharisees brought their tithes. They didn't rob God. Even so, obeying God only in lesser matters is not enough. Obedience in lesser matters is but the starting point.

Why do we make the test of authentic Christianity simplistic, external things like dancing and playing cards? Just consider this question: Is it easier to be known for your honor, trustworthiness, justness, and mercy, or to conform to externals. Is it easier to love your enemies or to not smoke, drink, or dance? In a sense, the latter are all minor things. The Bible says that the kingdom of God is not in eating and drinking. Yes, it's a sin to be gluttonous or to be drunk, but the issues that God has called us to be passionately concerned about are much more significant. We are to be concerned with integrity, justice, mercy, and helping a world that is in pain. It is all too simple to distort the biblical ethic by the kind of legalism that majors in minors.

One final type of legalism is what I like to call "loophole-ism." The Pharisees were masters of interpreting the law and creating loopholes so as to get around it. For example, the law said you couldn't go more than a Sabbath-day's journey on the Sabbath, a distance of about one mile from your residence. Legally, one's residence was where some of your personal possessions were stored. So, if the Pharisees wanted to make a six-mile trip on the Sabbath day, during the week they'd have a caravan trader take some of their toothbrushes and put one under a rock each mile along the way. By placing that toothbrush under the rock, the Pharisee technically established legal residence there. That way he would never travel more than a mile from his residence. His trip violated the point of the Sabbath-day's journey by getting around the law with a technicality.

God wants us to obey His law from a heart that desires to please Him. We must be careful of the distortion of legalism, but also the error in the other direction, antinomianism, to which we turn in the next chapter.

Chapter Five

THE DISTORTION
OF LAWLESSNESS

In the last chapter, we looked at the first of two distortions that would lead us away from a life of godliness and righteousness. We considered the various types of legalism that distort authentic righteousness. In this chapter, we will consider the opposite error, namely, the problem of *antinomianism*.

What is antinomianism? *Anti* is the Greek prefix that means "against," and *nomian* comes from the Greek word *nomos*, which means "law;" thus, antinomianism means "anti-lawism." As we considered the problem of legalism, you will recall that it was important to understand that there are several varieties of legalism. It's not good enough to simply have a blanket understanding of legalism. We need to be precise in our thinking and see the differences as they manifest themselves. The same is true of antinomianism. There are different kinds of antinomianism, and each has its own subtle variations and attractive dimensions.

The first type of antinomianism is called *libertinism*. Since our justification is by faith alone and not by the works of the law, a libertine Christian might think he is under grace and totally free from having to obey God's commandments. Libertinism becomes a license to sin, so it is really liberty gone astray. The libertine may be tempted to think that his love of sin and God's eagerness to forgive is a great combination. God gets to do what He loves and the sinner gets to do what he loves. A person of this inclination fails to remember what Paul wrote in the book of Romans: "What shall we say then? Are we to continue in sin that grace may abound?" (Rom. 6:1). Paul answers that rhetorical question by saying, "God forbid that we should ever arrive at a conclusion like that." Unfortunately, this is the philosophy of the libertine. He sees his redemption from the curse of the law as a license to sin.

Consider also what Peter said, "For this is the will of God, that by doing good you should put to silence the ignorance of foolish people. Live as people who are free, not using your freedom as a cover-up for evil, but living as servants of God"(1 Peter 2:15–16). It sounds almost contradictory when Peter describes us as free and servants of God at the same time. But it is only when we are in bondage to Christ that we understand true liberty. Peter warns against those who use their freedom as a license for wrongdoing.

A second type of antinomianism is what I call *gnostic spiritualism*. During the first and second centuries, one of the most dangerous rivals to the Christian faith was Gnosticism. The Gnostics took their name from the Greek word for knowledge—*gnosis*. They believed that they had access to special forms of knowledge that others did not have. They thought they had authority to recommend certain forms of non-Christian behavior because they presumed to possess higher knowledge that was secretive and esoteric.

We don't have card-carrying Gnostics in the twenty-first century in the same form they were found millennia ago, but the Gnostic heresy is still alive and well. In fact, the

Gnostic spirit of ethics is epidemic in Evangelical Christianity. But where do we see evidence of this Gnostic spirit?

Just consider how often you have heard people say, "The Spirit led me to do this or to do that." We have to be very cautious here. God the Holy Spirit does lead us, but the primary meaning of the leading of the Holy Spirit is not to lead us to marry this person or that person or to lead us to Cincinnati or Chicago. The primary place to which the Spirit leads us is to holiness and obedience. Sadly, many Christians put a cloak of spirituality around their ethical decisions so as to effectively stop voices of criticism before they're even heard.

Certainly, the Spirit lead us to certain specific life choices such as a spouse, a new job, or a new place to live. But it's all too easy to remove yourself from any discussion about the choices that you make by simply saying, "God is calling me to do . . ." Who wants to argue with God's call? This can easily become a sinful evasion of responsibility where we use spiritual language to remove ourselves from accountability in the Christian community. There are times when we should be required to give thoughtful reasons as to why we want to do whatever it is we want to do.

Importantly, the guidance of the Holy Spirit is not in itself antinomianism. It's not anti-law to be led by the Spirit of God; we're supposed to follow the leading of the Spirit of God. What becomes devastating is doing things that are clearly violating the revealed principles and precepts of the Word of God and then having the audacity to defend our actions by saying the Holy Spirit led us into it. I know one Christian man who became involved in a moral problem that was a direct violation of the law of God. He knew that was the case, but he was so caught up in it that his defense was that he had prayed about it and God had granted him an exception. That man was fooling himself and, at the same time, doing violence to the Holy Spirit.

God the Holy Spirit does not lead us to break His law. We are called to test the spirits. A spirit who is from God agrees with the testimony of the Holy Spirit, who has given us the Scriptures. We must be careful of this kind of spiritualism that confuses our desires with the leading of the Lord. It's a veiled form of antinomianism.

I call the third type of antinomianism *situationalism*. Maybe you've heard the familiar phrase *situational ethics*. This philosophy was developed by Joseph Fletcher. He sought to make love the highest norm above all others. He was searching for a middle road between the two dangers of legalism and antinomianism, and he declared that the only absolute was the absolute law to love. All other laws, he declared, are subject to the law of love and should be broken if a better and more loving course of action can be found. Fletcher wanted to find the best outcome of a given situation by holding up the law of love.

This may sound well and good, but this view has problems. We must never say that Scripture's other laws are negotiable or reducible to one ill-designed view of love. Fletcher said that we are supposed to do what *seems* right in a given situation. We are to do what love would demand that we do. But the Bible doesn't say what love *seems* to be; rather, it defines what love *is*.

Allow me to illustrate. Paul wrote to the Ephesians: "Therefore be imitators of God, as beloved children. And walk in love, as Christ loved us and gave himself up for us, a fragrant offering and sacrifice to God" (Eph. 5:1–2). Now consider the very next verse, "But sexual immorality and all impurity or covetousness must not even be named among you, as is proper among saints" (Eph. 5:3). The Apostle said to walk in love, but what does it mean to walk in love? It means you are never to be involved in sexual immorality. He attaches a prohibition against sexual immorality as a universal prohibition. This defines what love demands, but we only get half of that from Fletcher. If we follow Fletcher's reasoning, it might lead us to the oldest argument that men have used to seduce women: "If you love me, you will." We must know that if love is left uninformed and its content is given merely by what seems right to me according to my personal, subjective preference, the situation becomes the ultimate norm rather than the Word of God. God, however, tells us what love truly demands.

Situational ethics is clearly antinomian. By its own testimony, it reduces the law of God to one law, the law of love. The New Testament certainly focuses on love and says love is the summary of the law. Even Augustine made the statement, "Love God and do as you please." But when Augustine defined what he meant by that statement, he said that if you love God, you will be pleased by what pleases Him. How do you know what pleases God, except by careful study of the law of God? Jesus said, "If you love me, you will keep my commandments" (John 14:15). Commandments come out of love, and the Christian who is bound by the law of love is a Christian who recognizes the normative authority of the commandments of Jesus. That's my issue with the new morality. Who is Lord? Who has the right to impose obligations upon us? God may do it, God can do it, and God has done it.

Chapter Six

Degrees
of Sin

An important and practical question that we must address before we finish our look at building a Christian conscience is the question as to whether there are degrees of sin and of righteousness. There appears to be a great misunderstanding about biblical ethics in the secular culture. Not too long ago, I read an interesting essay written by a renowned psychiatrist who was distressed about Christianity. He expressed his concern that in his practice he dealt everyday with people who were neurotic, and at times psychotic, as a result of their inability to handle guilt. As an aside, have you ever stopped to think how many problems in psychiatry relate to the question of guilt? There's a sense in which a medical practitioner has to be concerned with ethics, the relationship between right and wrong, and the powerful impact of guilt on the human personality.

This particular psychiatrist wrote a critique of the ethical teachings of Jesus. Usually, those who are most hostile to Jesus, the church, and Christianity have good words for Jesus as an ethical teacher. They don't believe He's divine, nor that He's the Savior of the world, but they grant that He's the greatest ethical teacher who has ever lived. But not this doctor. He laid down the gauntlet and made it clear that Jesus was not a great teacher of ethics.

The psychiatrist directed his readers to the Sermon on the Mount and said that it is the crux of Jesus' ethical teaching. The doctor questioned why we would take Jesus' teaching seriously at all. Why, he asked, is Jesus a great moral teacher since He said that it is just as bad to lust after a woman as it is to commit adultery or that it's just as bad to hate somebody as it is to kill them? The psychiatrist claimed that such an ethic was foolishness. He wondered how a truly wise person could rank these different actions equally. Lust may be bad, but the consequences of it are truly different than actually committing adultery. The same is true for anger and murder. The psychiatrist was left dumbfounded as to why people elevate Jesus as a great ethical teacher.

At one point, I share the consternation of that psychiatrist. If Jesus of Nazareth had ever taught that adultery is no worse than lust and that murder is no worse than hate, I would be as astonished as the psychiatrist that anyone would revere the ethical teachings of Jesus. But the fact is that Jesus never taught that it is as bad to lust as it is to commit adultery or that it is as bad to be angry as it is to murder.

Why would someone come to the idea that Jesus taught that there are no distinctions? I think it comes from a simple misreading of the Sermon on the Mount. In that sermon, Jesus was dealing with the Pharisees and their teaching. He said, "You have heard that it was said to those of old, 'You shall not murder; and whoever murders will be liable to judgment.' But I say to you that everyone who is angry with his brother will be liable to judgment; whoever insults his brother will be liable to the council; and whoever says, 'You fool!' will be liable to the hell of fire" (Matt. 5:21–22).

Jesus also said, "You have heard that it was said, 'You shall not commit adultery.' But I say to you that everyone who looks at a woman with lustful intent has already committed adultery with her in his heart" (Matt. 5:27–28). Jesus actually never says that it's as bad to hate as it is to murder. Moreover, we can't legitimately infer that from His teachings. What was his point then?

Consider a continuum. On the left, one has the most heinous act, which would be the physical act of adultery. On the right, one would have the righteousness of true chastity. There are many behaviors that fall between these opposing poles. A man can kiss a woman who is not his wife. That's not adultery. It's not sexual intercourse. The relationship can progress through stages of deeper and deeper involvement sexually. The relationship may start as something innocent such as a righteous friendship, but the friendship can progress in stages in the direction of an illicit, unlawful relationship that culminates in the physical act of adultery. There are steps along the way between righteousness and the heinous act of adulterous intercourse. Lust is usually one of those steps. When lust is born in the mind, that's the first step towards moving in the direction of carrying out the fantasy that actually ends in adultery. The point Jesus made is that the law that God gives—"Thou shalt not commit adultery"—is not kept fully if one merely refrains from the physical act of adultery. When God forbids adultery, the full measure of that prohibition incorporates within it the whole complex of that sin, not only the actual act but all of the things that are a part of it. If you lust, Jesus said you have not fulfilled the whole measure of the law. That's a vital point for us to understand because otherwise, the scriptural ethic would make no sense.

Historically speaking, both Roman Catholicism and Protestantism have understood that there are degrees of sin. The Roman Catholic church makes a distinction between mortal and venial sin. The point of that distinction is that there are some sins so gross, heinous, and serious that the actual commission of those sins is mortal in the sense that it kills the grace of justification that resides in the soul of the believer. In their theology, not every sin is devastating to that degree. There are some real sins that are venial sins. These are less serious sins in terms of their consequences, but they don't have the justification-killing capacity that mortal sins have.

Many Evangelical Protestants have rejected the idea of degrees of sin because they know that the Protestant

Reformation rejected the Roman Catholic distinction between mortal and venial sins. As a result, they've jumped to the conclusion that there are no distinctions between sins in Protestantism.

We should return to the views of the Reformers themselves. John Calvin was an outspoken critic of the Roman Catholic Church and their distinction between mortal and venial sin. Calvin said that all sin is mortal in the sense that it deserves death. The book of James reminds us, "For whoever keeps the whole law but fails in one point has become accountable for all of it" (James 2:10). Even the slightest sin is an act of cosmic treason. We fail to feel the gravity of our actions to this degree, but it is true.

When I sin, I choose my will over the will of God Almighty. By implication I'm essentially saying that I'm more intelligent, wise, righteous, and powerful than God Himself. Calvin said that all sin is mortal in the sense that God could justifiably destroy each of us for the smallest sin we've committed. In fact, the penalty for sin was given the first day of human creation: "But of the tree of the knowledge of good and evil you shall not eat, for in the day that you eat of it you shall surely die" (Gen. 2:17). Yet God doesn't deal with us always according to justice. He deals with us according to grace, He allows us to live, and He moves to bring about our redemption. Calvin said that all sins are mortal in that we deserve death from them but that no sin is mortal in the sense that it can destroy our saving grace. We have to repent, yes, but the justifying grace that the Holy Spirit brings to us is not killed by our sin. Calvin and every one of the Reformers strenuously maintained that there is a difference between lesser sins and what they called gross and heinous sins.

This distinction is important for Christians to understand so that we can learn to live charitably with each other. The sin of pettiness, by which people begin to dwell on minor transgressions in the community, can tear the body of Christ apart. Great damage comes when it is fueled by the fire of gossip and slander. We are called to patience and tolerance towards the struggling failures of other Christians. It's not that we're called to be lax on sin, for there are certain sins listed in the New Testament that are serious and ought not be allowed in the church. Adultery is serious. Incest calls for ecclesiastical discipline. Drunkenness, murder, and fornication are repeatedly mentioned. These sins are so destructive that they call forth church discipline when they are manifested.

It's clear that we have different degrees of sin when we consider the warnings of Scripture. There are at least twenty-two references in the New Testament to degrees of rewards that are given to the saints in heaven. There are different levels, different rewards, and different roles in heaven. The Bible warns us against adding to the severity of our judgment. Jesus said to Pontius Pilate, "He who delivered me over to you has the greater sin" (John 19:11). Jesus measures and evaluates guilt, and with the greater guilt and greater responsibility comes the greater judgment. It's a motif that permeates the New Testament.

The idea of gradation of sin and reward is based upon God's justice. If I commit twice as many sins as another person, justice demands that the punishment fits the crime. If I've been twice as virtuous as another person, justice demands that I get more of a reward. God tells us that entrance into heaven will be only on the basis of the merit of Christ, but once we get to heaven, rewards will be dispensed according to works. Those who have been abundant in good works will receive an abundant reward. Those who have been derelict and negligent in good works will have a small reward in heaven. By the same token, those who have been grievous enemies of God will have severe torments in hell. Those who have been less hostile will have a lesser punishment at the hands of God. He is perfectly just, and when He judges, He will take into account all of the extenuating circumstances. Jesus said, "I tell you, on the day of judgment people will give account for every careless word they speak" (Matt. 12:36).

Why is it important for us to emphasize this point? Many times I've talked to men who struggle with lust and they say to themselves or to me, "I might as well go ahead and commit adultery because I'm already guilty of lust. I can't be in any worse shape in the sight of God, so I might as well finish the deed." I always answer, "Oh yes, you can be in much worse shape." The judgment of actual adultery will be much more severe than the judgment upon lust. God will deal with us at that level, and it's a foolish thing for a person who has committed a misdemeanor, to therefore say, "I'm already guilty; I might as well make it a felony." God forbid that we should think like that. If we do, we face the righteous judgment of God. We must keep this in mind as we seek to build a Christian conscience and a Christian character.

About the Author

Dr. R. C. Sproul is the founder and chairman of Ligonier Ministries, an international Christian education ministry based in Sanford, Florida. He also serves as co-pastor of Saint Andrew's Chapel, a Reformed congregation in Sanford, and as president of Reformation Bible College. His teaching can be heard around the world on the daily radio program *Renewing Your Mind*.

During his distinguished academic career, Dr. Sproul helped train men for the ministry as a professor at several theological seminaries.

He is the author of more than eighty books, including *The Holiness of God, Chosen by God, The Invisible Hand, Faith Alone, A Taste of Heaven, Truths We Confess, The Truth of the Cross*, and *The Prayer of the Lord*. He also served as general editor of *The Reformation Study Bible* and has written several children's books, including *The Prince's Poison Cup*.

Dr. Sproul and his wife, Vesta, make their home in Longwood, Florida.

Further your Bible study with *Tabletalk* magazine, another learning tool from R.C. Sproul.

....

Sign-up for a free, 3-month trial
of *Tabletalk* magazine
and get *The Holiness of God*
by R.C. Sproul for free.

Go online at TryTabletalk.com/CQ